The FM Legacy.

A Rock and Roll trivia Book.

By
Neil Fager

Copyright 2009.

This book is dedicated to:

My wonderful wife Marie, who has indulged me in this and many other flights of fancy.

My Hard Rock guitar playing son Alex, about whom I will be writing trivia questions some day.

And to the Reno Rock and Roll radio stations who have filled the airwaves with my inspiration. Thank you all.

"Welcome back my friends
To the show that never ends.
We're so glad you could attend.
Come inside! Come inside!

Karn Evil 9 1st impression, Pt 2.
Emerson, Lake and Palmer.

Introduction.

Welcome to "The FM Legacy. A Rock and Roll Trivia Book." The questions in this book are concerned with, as the title might suggest, the world of Rock and Roll music. The Songs, the Artists, their Albums and their History.

The first question in this trivia compendium is how to define Rock and Roll music. If you ask ten people to define Rock and Roll, you would end up with nine different definitions. (You always have that one Goober that agrees with everyone else.) Does the spectrum span from the Monkees to Metalica? What are the parameters?

For the purposes of this collection we are concerned primarily with the music you might hear on a "Classic Rock" radio station. However, we also include some peripheral Rock genera's that "Classic Rock" fans might also reasonably listen to. So, along with the Who, The Stones, and Aerosmith, you will find some Eighties Hair Bands, some Sixties Psychadelia, some Fifties Roots Rock as well as some contemporary artists.

I understand that these parameters might not please the purists, but hey, if you run across a question that you don't consider to be Rock and Roll, don't answer it. Skip to the next one. It will probably be close enough for you. And besides, in the search for 501 book worthy Rock trivia gems, even Olivia Newton-John starts to sound a little kick-ass.

But I digress.

Our conclusion is that you will find our Rock and Roll spectrum to be somewhat broad.

Secondly, I would like to mention the type of book this is not. It is certainly not a definitive work of Rock and Roll trivia. Even as I peruse it now I realize that there is so much material that I didn't cover.

Also, this is not a trivia contest of a quiz. There is no grading or point system separating the Rock Gods from the

Easy Listeners. What I consider to be a tough question may be simple to you. So if you came to this tome seeking some affirmation of your Rock trivia prowess, then you will have to keep your own scorecard.

This is the kind of book that you bring with you to the bonfire on the beach with your buddies. The kind that you argue about and chuckle over after a few cold ones. Think about it, you didn't find this book in the literature section. So, have fun with it.

That is the kind of book this is.

NF

1. What are that three generations of the 'Tostig' family named in the Elton John song "Levon?"

2. Name the four band members mentioned in the Creedence Clearwater Revival tune "Down On The Corner."

3. In the Grateful Dead song "Friend Of The Devil." in what western state did the narrator spend the night?

4. What color were the ten saxophones in the Neil Young And Crazy Horse song "Cinnamon Girl?"

5. What has happened to the butterfly in the Police offering "King Of Pain?"

6. In the Jethro Tull number "Bungle In The Jungle," where did "He who makes kittens," put the snakes?

7. What kind of 'Genius' is mentioned in the Styx ditty "Too Much Time On My Hands?"

1. Alvin, Levon and Jesus.

2. Willie, Rooster, Blinky and Poor Boy.

3. In Utah.

4. They were "Ten silver saxes."

5. It is "...Trapped in a spiders web."

6. "In the grass."

7. A "...Jet fuel genius."

8. It is mentioned in the Crosby, Stills and Nash song "Southern Cross" that the vessel in the song is on the "...Downhill run to Papaetee." Where is Papaetee?

9. In the Lynyrd Skynyrd song "Gimme Three Steps," how far away could you hear the narrator screaming as he headed out towards the door?

10. In "Don't Stand So Close To Me," a Police song about an older man with a thing for a school aged girl, Sting mentions "That book by Nabokov." What is 'that book?'

11. According to the Lynyrd Skynyrd song "That Smell," what is that smell?

12. In a Guns And Roses song, who has "...Eyes of the bluest skies?"

13. The Red Hot Chili Peppers sing that "She's a runner, rebel and a stunner." Who is she?

14. In a Led Zeppelin number Robert Plant tells us that "I don't know but I've been told..." Told what?

8. Tahiti.

9. A mile away.

10.'Lolita.'

11.The smell of death.

12."Sweet Child O' Mine."

13."Dani California."

14."A big legged woman ain't got no soul."

15. In the Stones "Honky tonk Woman," where did the narrator meet a "...Gin soaked, barroom queen..?"

16. According to Jethro Tull, who drew 'Cross Eyed Mary's' attention as "He" watched her through the railings as she played?

17. Who was the only performer to appear twice at the Woodstock Music and Art Fair in August of 1969?

18. Where does Steve Miller want the "Big Old Jet Airliner" to take him?

19. What historical event is depicted in the Mark Knophler song "Sailing To Philadelphia?"

20. In Boston's "More Than A Feeling," who does the singer see walking away?

21. In the Eric Clapton hit "Lay Down Sally," how long has he been waiting to talk to her?

15.Memphis.

16.Aqualung.

17.Country Joe McDonald. He appeared as a solo artist and with Country Joe And The Fish.

18.Nowhere it would seem. "It's here that I've got to stay."

19.The drawing of the Mason Dixon line.

20.Marianne.

21."...All night long..."

22. In the Queen anthem "We Are The Champions," what does Freddie Mercury thank us all for giving him?

23. In the Cream song "White Room," what does the singer see "...In her dark eyes?"

24. In the Steely Dan tune "My Old School," what kind of flowers were "...Growing outside her door?"

25. Deep Purple's hit "Smoke On The Water" takes place in what European country?

26. In the Dead tune "Truckin'," what did 'Sweet Jane's' diet consist of?

27. In a Green Day ditty, "Jimmy says it's better than air." What is *It*?

28. In the Who offering "I Can See For Miles And Miles," what famous landmarks can a man "...See on clearer days?"

22."...Fame and Fortune and everything that goes with it."

23.Yellow Tigers crouched in jungles.

24.Oleanders.

25.Switzerland.

26."...Reds, Vitamin C and cocaine." (All a friend can say is, 'Ain't it a shame.')

27.Novocaine.

28.The Eiffel Tower and the Taj Mahal.

29. The Who describe The Pinball Wizard as having what kind of wrist?

30. What was the only Frank Zappa number to reach the billboard Top Forty?

31. According to a 1985 Sting tune, what should you do if "...You love somebody?"

32. What kind of "Fly" does ZZ Top sing about in a 1986 song?

33. The Eagles "Witchy Woman" "...Drove herself to madness," with what?

34. What are the two rail lines mentioned by the Doobie Brothers in their tune "Long Train Running?"

35. Who drives the singers limousine in the Dr. Hook song "The Cover Of The Rolling Stone?"

29. He has a "Supple" wrist.

30. Valley Girl.

31. Set Them Free.

32. A "Velcro Fly."

33. "...A silver spoon." (Yes, that kind of spoon.)

34. "The Illinois Central and the Southern Central Freight."

35. It's his "...Poor old, gray hired daddy."

36. What literary work forms the basis of the Jefferson Airplane classic "White Rabbit?"

37. How does Eric Burdon describe himself in the War offering "Spill The Wine?"

38. In what number by the band War are we encouraged to "Take a little trip, Take a little trip, Take a little trip with me?"

39. In "It Don't Come Easy," Ringo Starr tells us that he "...Don't ask for much, I only want..." what?

40. How does the subject of the Bad Company song "Shooting Star" meet his demise?

41. In the weird Al Yankovic classic "Yoda," what British invasion era Rock band is he doing a parody of? And an extra point if you can name the song.

42. What character from The Lord Of The Rings trilogy is mentioned in the Led Zeppelin tune "Ramble On?"

36.Alice In Wonderland.

37.As an "Over fed, Long haired, leaping Gnome."

38."Low Rider."

39.Trust.

40.A drug overdose. ("Bottle of whiskey, sleeping tablets by his head.")

41.The band is The Kinks and the song is "Lola."

42.Gollum. ("The evil one.")

43. In George Thoroughgoods rambling rejoinder, "1 Bourbon, 1 Scotch and 1 Beer,"the bartender announces "Last call for alcohol" at what time?

44. According to Jimi Hendrix, where did Joe go after he shot his old lady?

45. Lynyrd Skynyrd mentions what national political scandal in their anthem "Sweet Home Alabama?"

46. In the Rod Stewart smash "Maggie May," what does he ponder stealing from his daddy?

47. In the Rolling Stones ditty "Shattered," what are people directing traffic in New York City dressed in?

48. In what Rolling Stones track does Mick Jagger exclaim, "I think her engines are permanently stalled?"

49. In George Harrison's brilliant Beatles classic "While My Guitar Gently Weeps," who is it that actually plays the weeping guitar?

43.At three o'clock. (No word weather that's AM or PM.)

44."Way down south to Mexico way."

45.Watergate.

46.His pool cue.

47.Plastic bags.

48."She's So Cold."

49.Eric Clapton.

50. The assassination of what legendary American is recounted in U2's "Pride, In The Name Of Love?"

51. Why do people think the singer is insane according to Black Sabbath's "Paranoid?"

52. Cheap Trick bemoans that "They're waiting for me, they're looking for me. Every single night!" Who are they?

53. In the Steppenwolf track "Born To Be Wild," the singer mentions a certain kind of thunder. What kind of thunder?

54. Anthony Topham, Eric Clapton, Jeff Beck and Jimmy Page were all guitarists in various incarnations of what legendary British band?

55. In a Pretenders tune, Chrissie Hynde went back to Ohio to find "The pretty country side had been paved down the middle..." by whom?

56. What is the next line in this sequence from Steppenwolf's "Magic Carpet Ride." "Close your eyes girl. Look inside girl..."

50. The Reverend Dr. Martin Luther King Jr.

51. Because "I am frowning all the time."

52. The Dream Police.

53. "Heavy metal thunder."

54. The Yardbirds.

55. "A government that had no pride."

56. "...Let the sound take you away."

57. They evolved from The Yardbirds into The New Yardbirds, then into what legendary band?

58. In 1985, Motley Crue did a cover of the teenage anthem "Smokin' In The Boys Room." Who scored a top ten hit with the original version?

59. The opening line of Paul McCartney's "Uncle Albert/Admiral Halsey" has Paul apologizing to Uncle Albert for something. Why is he apologizing?

60. What Dire Straits ballad has a young girl wearing a Walkman with the headphones on roller skating blissfully through evening traffic?

61. Special Discussion Question.
    We all know Rock and Roll when we hear it, but what qualities define Rock and Roll?

62. What James Bond film did Paul McCartney and Wings perform the title song for?

63. In the Five Man Electrical Band ditty "Signs," what does the sign say the penalty is for trespassing?

57.Led Zeppelin.

58.Brownsville Station.

59.Because "...We haven't done a bloody thing all day."

60.Skateaway.

61.It's a Special Discussion Question. What are you looking here for?

62.Live and Let Die.

63.To be "...Shot on sight."

64. What 'Sister' was the subject of 1975 hit for the band America?

65. In the Animals song "We Gotta Get Out Of This Place," what does Eric Burdon say that his "Daddy" is doing in bed?

66. According to the Beatles "A Day In The Life," how many holes does it take to fill the Albert Hall?"

67. In "When You're Strange," the Doors tell us that the "Streets" take on a certain quality "When you're down." What quality?

68. In the Eddie Money hit "Take Me Home Tonight" he informs us that it's "...Just like Ronnie said." Ronnie who?

69. In the Zombies classic slice of psychedelia "Time Of The Season," what question follows the line "Whats your name?"

70. The Moody Blues tell us that "If you'll just come with me you'll see the beauty of..." What?

64. Sister Golden Hair.

65. "A dying."

66. 4000.

67. "The streets are uneven..."

68. Veronica "Ronnie" Spector. Lead singer of the Ronettes.

69. "Who's your daddy?"

70. "Tuesday afternoon."

71. In "Being For The Benefit Of Mr. Kite," who dances the waltz?

72. In Steve Miller's "Take The Money And Run," where did Billy Joe and Bobbi Sue run into a "...Great big hassle?"

73. In Alice Cooper's "No More Mr. Nice Guy," who punches him in the nose?

74. According to the Beatles "A Day In The Life," where were the holes?

75. What group performs with Mr. Kite in the Beatles song that bears his name?

76. In George Thorougood's "Bad To The Bone," who warned "Leave this one alone?"

77. What band brought us yodeling gibberish and smoking guitars with the number "Hocus Pocus?"

71. Henry The Horse. Of course.

72. "Old El Paso."

73. The Reverend Smith.

74. Blackburn Lancashier.

75. The Hendersons.

76. The head nurse.

77. Focus.

78. Pink Floyd's "Wish You Were Here" poses the quandary "Would you exchange a walk on part in a war, for..." what?

79. What is the intro to the Boston song "Long Time" called?

80. Who portrayed the "Acid Queen" in the film version of the Rock opera "Tommy?"

81. What amusement game manufacturer is mentioned in the Who song "Pinball Wizard?"

82. Edgar Winter named a legendary instrumental hit after what literary mad scientist?

83. In a 1967 hit album, Jefferson Airplane offered us what kind of 'Pillow'?

84. For what group was Janis Joplin the vocalist?

78."...A lead roll in a cage."

79."Foreplay."

80.Tina Turner.

81. Bally.

82.Frankenstein.

83.A "Surrealistic Pillow."

84.Big Brother And The Holding Company.

85. In the Joe Walsh introspective classic "Life's Been Good," he says he's got him an office. What is it called?

86. According to a Pink Floyd song, what kind of sarcasm is Not needed in the classroom?

87. Name the happy couple in the Beatles hit Ob-La-Di Ob-La-Da.

88. What night is "All right for fighting," according to Elton John?

89. What actress was nominated for an Oscar for her performance in the film version of the Rock opera "Tommy?"

90. What brand of champagne is kept "...In a pretty cabinet," in the Queen song "Killer Queen?"

91. "Let It Be" was the last Beatles album released. What was the last Beatles album recorded?

85."Records On The Wall."

86.Dark sarcasm.

87.Desmond and Molly Jones.

88.Saturday Night.

89.Ann Margaret.

90.Moet & Chandon.

91.Abbey Road.

92. What baseball position is John Fogarty ready to play according to a 1985 hit?

93. What legendary British band was originally known as "The High Numbers?"

94. What are the lyrics in the refrain of the Van Halen selection "Eruption?"

95. What type of eye wear is recommended in a ZZ Top song?

96. What is Meat Loaf left waiting for at the conclusion of "Paradise By The Dashboard Lights?"

97. What did the lady form Majorca Spain offer Ringo in "The No No Song?"

98. What kind of pie is mentioned in Paul McCartney's "Uncle Albert/ Admiral Halsey?"

92.Center Field.

93.The Who.

94.None, it is an instrumental.

95."Cheap Sunglasses."

96.The end of time. (To hurry up and arrive!)

97."...A ten pound bag of cocaine."

98.A "Butter Pie."

99. According to "Honky Tonk Woman," who got "Laid" in New York City?

100. What tempo of 'Ride' did Fog Hat offer us with one of their songs?

101. What psychedelic San Francisco group gave us "White Bird?"

102. In the Who classic "Wont Get Fooled Again," how is the new 'Boss?'

103. What "Zone" did the band Golden Earring step into with a 1983 hit?

104. According to Styx, who pleads, "Give ma a job, give me security. Give me a chance to survive.?"

105. In what Pink Floyd song is it noted that "The sun is the same in a relative way, but your older?"

99.A divorcee.

100. A "Slow Ride."

101. It's A Beautiful Day.

102. "Same as the old boss."

103. The "Twilight Zone."

104. The "Blue Collar Man."

105. Time.

106. Who did the band "The Knack" have the hots for in a 1979 number one smash?

107. In what Fastball song will they "...Never get hungry, they'll never get old and gray?"

108. Before the Silver Bullet Band, what was Bob Seger's group known as?

109. The group Kansas tells us in the song "Dust In The Wind" that "Nothing lasts forever but..." But what?

110. In a David Bowie offering, what does Ground Control say is wrong with Major Tom's spaceship?

111. in a Guns And Roses song, Axl Rose croons that he "Used to love her..." but he had to do something. What?

112. Ray Manzarek, Robby Krieger and John Densmore round out what famous Rock foursome?

106. "My Sharona."

107. "The Way."

108. The Bob Seger System.

109. "The earth and sky."

110. His 'Circuit's' dead.

111. He "...Had to kill her."

112. The Doors.

113. The only number one Billboard hit for the band The Guess Who was a song about what nationality of woman?

114. Who did the Beatles reveal to be "The Walrus" in the song "Glass Onion?"

115. What time is it said to be at the beginning of the Golden Earring song "The Twilight Zone?"

116. Was Jimi Hendrix right handed or left handed?

117. Where does Bob Seger find "The pool halls, the hustlers and the losers?"

118. What does Billy Idol say she wants with her "Rebel Yell?"

119. What is the one word name of the Red Hot Chili Peppers bassist?

113. An "American Woman."

114. Paul McCartney.

115. 2 am.

116. He was left handed.

117. Down on "Main Street."

118. "More, More, More!"

119. Flea.

120. Who was the left handed Beatle?

121. According to the band America, what does the desert induce you to forget?

122. Who was the featured guitarist on the David Bowie song "Lets Dance?"

123. What was the Beatles second movie?

124. Where does Levon spend his days counting his money?

125. Who was John Lennon's first wife?

126. What Seattle hard Rockers sing about their "Jet City Woman?"

120. Paul McCartney.

121. Your name.

122. Stevie Ray Vaughn.

123. Help!

124. "In the garage by the motorway."

125. Cynthia Powell.

126. Queensryche.

127. "Something," "Come Together" and "Maxwell's Silver Hammer." Name the album.

128. Journey lead guitarist Neal Schon was a protege of what guitar legend?

129. What was Janis Joplin's only Billboard number one hit?

130. When not serving in the Australian senate, for what band is Peter Garrett the lead singer?"

131. In the Dire Straits ditty "Money for Nothing," how much did the 'chicks' cost?

132. In a 1979 Police song, Sting beseeches a prostitute not to ply her trade. What was that prostitute's name?

133. Eleven people were trampled to death in a rush for "Festival" seating before a 1979 "Who" concert in what city?

127. Abbey Road. (The Beatles.)

128. Carlos Santana.

129. "Me And Bobby McGee."

130. Midnight Oil.

131. They were free.

132. Roxanne.

133. Cincinnati.

134. In the Boston ballad "Rock And Roll Band," the band was 'discovered' while playing for a week where?

135. Who is Charlie Watts?

136. Crosby, Stills, Nash and Young chronicled the deaths of four young people on the campus of what Ohio university?

137. "Funeral For A Friend/Love Lies Bleeding," Saturday Night's Alright For Fighting" and Benny And The Jets." Name the album.

138. Who was the original singer for the band Genesis?

139. In what Police number is Sting, "...Too full to swallow my pride?"

140. In the Pink Floyd song "Run Like Hell," what happens if they "...Catch you in the back seat trying to pick her locks?"

134. Rhode Island.

135. Drummer for the Rolling Stones.

136. Kent State.

137. Goodbye Yellow Brick Road.

138. Peter Gabriel.

139. "Can't Stand Loosing You."

140. "They'll send you back to mother in a cardboard box."

141. At what venue was a young concert goer stabbed and kicked to death during a Rolling Stones concert in December 1969?

142. What are the names of the three grandchildren in the Beatles number "When I'm Sixty Four?"

143. What Bruce Springsteen song did Manfred Mann's Earth Band take to number one on the Billboard charts in 1976?

144. What were the Kinks tired of waiting for in a 1965 song?

145. Name the Doctor that KISS was calling for in a 1977 hit.

146. What kind of 'Vision' did Foreigner have in a 1978 hit song?

147. What guest artist played the pedal steel guitar on the Crosby, Stills, Nash and Young song "Teach Your Children?"

141. Altamont Motor Speedway, California.

142. Vera, Chuck and Dave.

143. "Blinded By The Light."

144. You.

145. "Doctor Love."

146. "Double Vision."

147. Jerry Garcia.

148. Who played the sax solo in the Foreigner tune "Urgent?"

149. With what very active hobby does Hard Rocker Billy Squier get high. Very high?

150. To whom is Bruce Springsteen singing in the song "Born To Run?"

151. Bob Seger gives us an honest portrayal of life on the road in what classic offering?

152. Mott The Hoople's anthem "All The Young Dudes," was written by what what famous 'Glam' Rocker?

153. Who is "Jigsaw Jimmy" better known as in a Motley Crue track?

154. What dubious royal residence did George Harrison take us to in a 1977 Hit?

148. Jr. Walker. (Formerly of Jr. Walker And The All Stars.)

149. Mountain climbing.

150. Wendy.

151. "Turn The Page."

152. David Bowie.

153. "Dr. Feelgood."

154. "Crackerbox Palace."

155. Name Jimi Hendrix's only Billboard top 40 hit.

156. What Heart tune was rumored to be about Charles Manson?

157. What kind of 'Lady' was the subject of a 1970 Sugarloaf hit?

158. What group opined in 1972 that "The World Is A Ghetto?"

159. Who sang lead for Ronny Montrose in the 1970's?

160. Denny Laine, a guitarist with Paul McCartney's Wings, was the original lead singer of what progressive Rock group?

161. William Bailey is better known as what Hard Rock front man?

155. "All Along The Watchtower."

156. "Magic Man." (Which was actually about Dennis Wilson of the Beach Boys.)

157. She was a "Green-Eyed Lady."

158. War.

159. Sammy Hagar.

160. The Moody Blues.

161. Axl Rose.

162. Before Rod Argent formed a solo project, he played keyboards in what undead band?

163. From what multiple handicaps did "Tommy" suffer?

164. Van Halen put a Hard Rock twist on what Roy Orbison classic?

165. What brand of camera is mentioned in the Paul Simon confessional "Kodachrome?"

166. From what establishment can you "...Check out any time you like, but you can never leave?"

167. George Berger is one of the lead characters in what Rock musical?

168. According to ZZ Top, what will you find in "...That shack outside La Grange?"

162. The Zombies.

163. He was deaf, dumb and blind.

164. "Pretty Woman."

165. A Nikon camera.

166. The "Hotel California."

167. Hair.

168. "A lot of nice girls."

169. Who is Joe Perry?

170. What Procol Harum staple has it's melody based on the Bach cantata "Sleepers Awake?"

171. In a Styx number, why "Is it any wonder I'm null and void?"

172. What group gave us the story of a "Lucky Man." So lucky, in fact, that he got to die for his country and his king?

173. What manner of female made "The Rockin' world go 'round," according to a Queen song?

174. "The Song Is Over," "Behind Blue Eyes" and "Wont Get Fooled Again." Name the album.

175. In the Toto hit "Africa," what mountain is described as "Rising like Olympus above the Serengeti?"

169. The lead guitarist for the band Aerosmith.

170. "A Whiter Shade Of Pale."

171. Because, "I've got Too Much Time On My Hands."

172. Emerson, Lake and Palmer.

173. "Fat Bottomed Girls."

174. Who's Next. (The Who.)

175. Mt. Kilimanjaro.

176. Who did lead vocal duties for the group Bad Company?

177. "A girl named Linda Lou," appears in what Lynyrd Skynyrd song?

178. Who is Reginald Dwight better known as?

179. Name the only album from blues Rock super group Derek And The Dominoes.

180. Brian May, John Deacon and Roger Taylor round out what British 'Glam' Rock foursome?

181. What kind of love is driving Steve Miller mad and making him crazy?

182. Who was the lead vocalist for the band Steppenwolf?

51

176. Paul Rogers.

177. "Gimme' Three Steps."

178. Elton John.

179. "Layla And Other Assorted Love Songs."

180. Queen.

181. "Jungle Love."

182. John Kay.

183. Who advised us to "Take The Long Way Home" in a 1979 song?

184. According to their 1980 hit, what was The J. Geils Band's descriptive opinion of love?

185. What Rock guitar virtuoso was born in Autlan de Navarro, Mexico in July of 1947?

186. "My Hometown," "Glory Days, and "I'm On Fire." Name the album.

187. Special Discussion Question.
Was Ringo Starr the luckiest person of the 20th century? Talk this one out. See what you think.

188. What rock group decided in a 1981 track that "The waiting is the hardest part?"

189. Where did Lou Reed's Velvet Underground entreat us to take a 'walk,' in a 1973 song?

183. Supertramp.

184. "Love Stinks."

185. Carlos Santana.

186. Born In The U.S.A. (Bruce Springsteen.)

187. It's a Special Discussion Question. You won't find any answers here.

188. Tom Petty and the Heartbreakers.

189. "...On The Wild Side."

190. They're an Athens Georgia Rock quartet named for a specific stage in the sleep cycle. Who are they?

191. Tom Scholts and Brad Delp formed the core of what east coast Rock powerhouse?

192. Who is guitarist Saul Hudson better known as?

193. What Sammy Hagar hit lamented the rather conservative national speed limit back in 1984?

194. Before being discovered by legendary promoter Bill Graham and hitting the Rock music big time, what was Eddie Money's profession?

195. What Scottish Hard Rockers poured out their relationship angst in the anthem "Love Hurts?"

196. What Detroit Hard Rocker once fronted The Amboy Dukes?

190. R.E.M.

191. Boston.

192. Slash.

193. "I Cant Drive 55."

194. He was a New York City police officer.

195. Nazareth.

196. Ted Nugent.

197. Who worked at the Abbey Road recording studios engineering such as Pink Floyd's "Dark Side Of The Moon' and The Beatles "Abbey Road' before starting his own "Project?"

198. What Hard Rock quartet did the 'Unskinny Bop" in 1990?

199. What "sharp" moniker is Gorden Sumner better known by?

200. Roger Waters, David Gilmour, Rick Wright and Nick Mason make up what progressive Rock group?

201. What is Ringo Starr's real name?

202. What ailment did Ted Nugent suffer from according to a 1977 ditty?

203. Under what name did Creedence Clearwater Revival record before they became Creedence Clearwater Revival?

197. Alan Parsons.

198. Poison.

199. Sting.

200. Pink Floyd.

201. Richard Starkey.

202. "Cat Scratch Fever."

203. The Golliwogs.

204. If you churn Eric Clapton, Ginger Baker and Jack Bruce together, what do you get?

205. What team sport is referenced in the Joe Walsh number "Rocky Mountain Way?"

206. What is the next line in the sequence from the Stones song "She's So Cold?" "I'm the burnin' bush, I'm the burnin 'fire..."

207. What highway did the band America take us down in 1972?

208. What Detroit group took us on a "Journey To The Center Of The Mind?"

209. Where was "The House Of The Rising Sun?"

210. What band insisted that "You Ain't Seen Nothing Yet" in a 1974 hit?

204. Cream.

205. Baseball.

206. "I'm the bleedin' volcano!"

207. "Ventura Highway."

208. The Amboy Dukes.

209. New Orleans.

210. Bachman-Turner Overdrive.

211. Bad Company's Paul Rogers and Mick Ralphs had previously performed together in what band?

212. What Badfinger classic was written by Paul McCartney and featured in the film "The Magic Christian?"

213. The narrative in the Grateful Dead song "Friend Of The Devil" originates in what western city.

214. What Fleetwood Mac song was the theme song of the 1992 Clinton presidential campaign?

215. Name the band featured in the Jonathan Demme concert film "Stop Making Sense."

216. What was the name of the Beatles drummer replaced by Ringo Starr in 1962?

217. In a 1983 hit, what did ZZ Top try to convince us that every girl was crazy about?

211. Free.

212. "Come And Get It."

213. Reno.

214. "Don't Stop."

215. The Talking Heads.

216. Pete Best.

217. A "Sharp Dressed Man."

218. The Lynyrd Skynyrd classic "Sweet Home Alabama" includes a line about "...The Governor." Who was the governor of Alabama when that song was released?

219. What baseball hall of famer porvided the play by play voice in the tender Meatloaf ballad "Paradise By The Dashboard Lights?"

220. What 1984 Van Halen hit shares it's name with a central American country?

221. In a Bryan Addams song, when were the days that he considered to be "The best days of my life?"

222. Led Zeppelin was the subject of what eccentric concert film?

223. From what island nation do the Rockers AC/DC hail?

224. What character in the song "All Along The Watchtower" said "There must be some kind of way out of here?"

218. George Wallace.

219. Phil Rizzuto.

220. Panama.

221. Back in the "Summer Of '69."

222. "The Song Remains The Same."

223. Australia.

224. The Joker. He said it to the Thief.

225. What did the Jefferson Airplane suggest we "find" in a 1967 hit?

226. How long did Jim Morrison live?

227. Three Dog Night warned us of 'His' coming in a a 1969 tune. Who's coming?

228. In a Warren Zevon number, "A little old lady got mutilated late last night." Who were the likely culprits?

229. Crosby, Stills and Nash's "Suite: Judy Blue Eyes" was written as an ode to whom?

230. In John Cougar Mellencamp's "Jack And Diane," what were they "Suckin' on..." outside the "...Tastee Freeze?"

231. What took place on Max Yasgur's farm in upstate New York on August 15th through the 17th, 1969?

225. "Somebody To Love."

226. 27 years.

227. Eli.

228. "Werewolves Of London."

229. Judy Collins.

230. "Chili Dogs."

231. The Woodstock Music And Art Fair.

232. According to Thin Lizzy's "The Boys Are Back In Town." what is going to happen tonight down at "...Dino's Bar and Grill?"

233. How many "Na Na's" did Steve Perry and his Journey-Mates sing at the end of "Lovin', Touchin', Squeezing?"

234. In a 1973 novelty, The band Dr. Hook told us that they could have or do just about anything. Except... what?

235. "Raven hair, ruby lips. Sparks fly from her fingertips." Just who was this chick that the Eagles were singing about in 1972?

236. Who was "...Just alright," with the Doobie Brothers in a 1973 offering?

237. Robert Allen Zimmerman is better known as what folk Rock icon?

238. What kind of "Magic" did E.L.O. Sing about in a 1976 track?

232. "The drinks will flow and blood will spill."

233. 154. (That's seven rounds with 22 "Na Na's" per round. No, really! Count 'em yourself.)

234. Get their picture "...On the cover of the Rolling Stone."

235. "Witchy Woman.

236. Jesus.

237. Bob Dylan.

238. Strange Magic.

239. What movie icon did David Essex encourage us to see "...Shake on the movie screen" in his enigmatic offering "Rock On?"

240. What Texas blues Rockers wanted to know if they were "Tuff Enuff"in 1986?

241. While still attending Bard College in New York, Donald Fagen and Walter Becker, (Soon to be of Steely Dan fame,) formed a band with what future comic actor as their drummer? (P.S. This is the most obscure question in this entire book.)

242. "Kashmir," "Houses Of The Holy" and "Custard Pie." Name the album.

243. According to a Beatles song, "When it gets dark you tow my heart away." Who would do such a thing?

244. Who did Eric Clapton have in mind when he wrote the Derek And The Dominoes classic "Layla?"

245. Did Ozzy Osborne really bite the head off of a bat during a concert?

239. Jimmy Dean. (James Dean.)

240. The Fabulous Thunderbirds.

241. Chevy Chase.

242. Physical Graffiti.

243. "Lovely Rita, Meter Maid."

244. The song was written for Patty Boyd, the then wife of the Beatles George Harrison.

254. Yes. During a January 1982 show. Apparently he didn't think it was real.

246. The title of a 2004 U2 album mentions dismantling something. What?

247. What Red Hot Chili Pepper release was a two disc set with one disc labeled "Jupiter" and one disc labeled "Mars?"

248. What Rush tune sings the praises of the open radio airwaves?

249. What Blue Oyster Cult favorite encourages us to be unafraid of death?

250. In the song "Julia" from the Beatles "White Album," of whom was John Lennon singing?

251. What was the title of the Doors second album?

252. What British band warned us of an impending nighttime jailbreak?

246. An Atomic Bomb.

247. "Stadium Arcadium."

248. "The Spirit Of Radio."

249. "Don't Fear The Reaper."

250. His mother.

251. "Strange Days." (1967.)

252. Thin Lizzy.

253. Burton Cummings, Randy Bachman and Bob Ashley formed the core of what Canadian Rock band?

254. What event caused the demise of the mighty Led Zeppelin?

255. What San Francisco bay area band assembled the album "Cosmo's Factory?"

256. In a Dire Straits track, Jesus is out on a hunger strike and he's "...Dying by degrees." What affliction does he have?

257. "Cross Eyed Mary," "Locomotive Breath" and "Up To Me." Name the album?

258. According to a Genesis tune, just where *does* the lamb lie down?

259. In a 1978 number, Robert Palmer told his Doctor that "No pill's gonna cure my ill." Whatever was he suffering from?

253. The Guess Who.

254. The unfortunate death of drummer John Bonham on September 25th, 1980.

255. Creedence Clearwater Revival.

256. "Industrial Disease."

257. "Auqalung." (Jethro Tull.)

258. "On Broadway."

259. "A Bad Case Of Loving You."

260. In what 1981 song does Greg Kihn inform us, "We had broken up for good just an hour before."

261. Name the brothers that formed the core of the Brit Rockers "The Kinks."

262. Name the Fleetwood Mac hit that was recorded live at Dodger Stadium with the accompaniment of the USC Trojan marching band.

263. Before he had 'Come Alive' as a solo artist, he helped form the band Humble Pie at the age of 19. Who is he?

264. What Glenn Frey solo offering tells us of "...The politics of contraband?"

265. According to a 1985 song, where did John Cougar Mellencamp believe that he would probably be buried?

266. The Wilson sisters were the life blood of what popular 70's-80's hit makers?

260. The appropriately named "The Breakup Song."

261. Brothers Ray and Dave Davies.

262. "Tusk."

263. Peter Frampton.

264. "Smugglers Blues."

265. A "Small Town."

266. Heart.

267. Jimmy Page, Paul Rogers, Chris Slade and Tony Franklin joined forces as what "Radioactive" super group in 1985?

268. After what classical composer did Eddie Van Halen name his son?

269. "461 Ocean Boulevard" was a hit album for Eric Clapton in the mid 70's. What was the significance of that address?

270. What gimmick did the Who use to punctuate their live performances?

271. In what 1974 hit did Grand Funk Railroad ask, rhetorically, "Can I get a witness?"

272. Before forming the band The Eagles, Don Henley and Glenn Frey were part of the backup band for what singer?

273. Who was killed in a plane crash on February 3rd, 1959, the day the music died according to Don Mclean?

267. The Firm.

268. Wolfgang Amedeus Mozart.

269. It was the address of the house in Miami that he lived in at the time. The house was also featured in the album cover photo.

270. They would destroy their instruments.

271. "Some Kind Of Wonderful."

272. Linda Ronstadt.

273. Buddy Holly, Richie Valens and J.P. Richardson (The Big Bopper.). Any of those names are acceptable.

274. Call him by his real name of Willem Wolfe Broad and he will probably flash his trademark sneer at you. Who is he better known as?

275. According to the band Iron Butterfly, what was the original title of their psychedelic classic "In-A-Gadda-Da-Vida?"

276. Before he took over lead vocal duties for the Jefferson Starship and later just The Starship, Mickey Thomas voiced the song "Fooled Around And Fell In Love" for whom?

277. Apart from being the lead vocalist for Jethro Tull, what instrument does Ian Anderson play?

278. Before forming her own band, The Blackhearts, she was the guitarist with the female band The Runaways. Who is she?

279. In an Elton John song, "...I'm not the man they think I am at home. Oh no, no, no." Who am I?

280. What was the name of the Salvation Army children's home, immortalized in a Beatles song, where John Lennon played as a child?

274. Billy Idol.

275. "In The Garden Of Eden."

276. Elvin Bishop.

277. The Flute.

278. Joan Jett.

279. "I'm a Rocket Man."

280. "Strawberry Fields."

281. What tune about an absent female produced hits for both The Zombies and Carlos Santana?

282. In what Elton John number one hit song does he sing of a 6'3" Jamaican prostitute?

283. In 1968 the Beatles formed Apple Records as part of their Apple Corps. Who was the first artist they signed to Apple Records?

284. "Weird" Al Yankovic first garnered attention for his parody number "Another One Rides The Bus." What Rock staple is this tune a parody of?

285. Though no one could truly replace the force of nature that was Keith Moon, who did take over as drummer of The Who when Moon died?

286. What kind of "Truckin'" did Deep Purple do in 1972?

287. One of the most prolific artists of any genera, how many albums did Frank Zappa release?

281. "She's Not There."

282. "Island Girl."

283. James Taylor.

284. "Anther One Bites The Dust," by Queen.

285. Kenney Jones.

286. "Space Truckin'."

287. 42. (If you got this one right, all I can say is "Damn!")

288. What Randy Newman penned, Three Dog Night song tells of "...The craziest party that could ever be?"

289. In what classic Who song does Roger Daltrey sing of the "Teenage Wasteland?"

290. In a 1967 song, the Jefferson Airplane told us of this adjective laden 'Lover'. What kind of 'Lover'?

291. According to a Humble Pie number, "Black Napalese, it's got you week in the knees." What is "Black Napalese?"

292. In the song "Red House," Jimi Hendrix hasn't been home to see his baby in how long?

293. Lynyrd Skynyrd sings that this object "Ain't good for nothing but put a man six feet in a hole."What do *they* call this object?

294. In "Running On Empty," Jackson Browne describes himself at two different ages. What are those ages?

288. "Mama Told Me. (Not To Come.)

289. "Baba O'Riley."

290. A "Plastic, Fantastic Lover."

291. It is a form of Hashish.

292. "99 and ½ days."

293. "Mr. Saturday Night Special."

294. 17 and 21.

295. Where did Black Sabbath tell us that Iron Man was "...Turned to steel?"

296. Who provides Cheap Tricks lead vocals?

297. In Alice Cooper's "Schools Out," what is the next line in the sequence? "Schools out for summer. Schools out forever..."

298. What group gave us a Rocking version of the Ledbelly blues classic "Black Betty?"

299. What popular progressive Rock band hails from Topeka?

300. In the Elton John song "Daniel," who is Daniel in relation to the songs narrator?

301. In what Rush offering are we warned "Be cool or be cast out?"

295. "In the great magnetic field."

296. Robin Zander.

297. "Schools been blown to pieces!"

298. Ram Jam.

299. Kansas. Appropriately enough.

300. His older brother.

301. Subdivisions.

302. Dave Grohl rose form Nirvana's ashes to help found what current hard Rockers?

303. In the Faces offering "Stay With Me," what color are 'Rita's' "...Lips, hair and fingernail?"

304. Special Discussion Question.
Who do you think would have had a greater influence on Rock music if they were still alive today, Jimi Hendrix or Jim Morrison? Give it both thought and lively debate.

305. In what Steppenwolf track does John Kay confess that he has "...Smoked a lot of grass, and I've popped a lot of pills?"

306. What are the ultimate fates of the "Castles Made Of Sand" according to Hendrix?

307. What manner of 'Fantasy' did Bad Company have in 1979?

308. On how many original Van Halen albums, not best of compilations, did David Lee Roth appear?

302. The Foo Fighters.

303. Red.

304. I know what I think, but what d you think?

305. "The Pusher."

306. They alternately Fall, Melt and Slip into the sea.

307. A "Rock And Roll Fantasy."

308. Six.

309. Roy Orbison recorded with what supergroup before leaving us in 1988?

310. What is Ozzy Osborne's real first name? No, it isn't Ozzy.

311. What Eagle alumni contributed the number "All Night Long" to the Country and Western flick "urban Cowboy?"

312. In what 1966 tune do the Kinks complain "My girlfriend's run off with my car and went back to her Ma and Pa."

313. "Shout It Out Loud," "Beth" and "Detroit Rock City." Name the album.

314. What was Ringo offered by the man from Nashville Tennessee in "The No No song?"

315. Before forming Fleetwood Mac, John McVie and Mick Fleetwood were members of what legendary British blues band?

309. The Traveling Wilburys.

310. John.

311. Joe Walsh.

312. "Sunny Afternoon."

313. Destroyer. (KISS.)

314. Some Moonshine whisky.

315. John Mayall's Bluesbreakers.

316. For whom did Paul write the Beatles anthem "Hey Jude?"

317. What city is believed to be destroyed in a 1977 Blue Oyster Cult number?

318. In the Stones song "Miss You," Mick is encouraged to come around to the square because there are certain people "...Just dying to meet you." Who are these people?

319. In Steely Dan's "Do It Again," what kind of cards make you money?

320. The Zeppelin song "D'yer Mak'er" was their Rock and Roll interpretation of what musical genera?

321. According to George Thorogood, "I make a rich woman beg, I'll make a good woman steal, I'll make an old woman blush and I'll make a young girl squeal." Why?

322. In what Bob Seger smash does he show his disdain for both Disco and Tango music?

316. John Lennon's son Julian.

317. Tokyo.

318. Puerto Rican girls.

319. Black cards.

320. Reggae.

321. Because I'm "Bad To The Bone."

322. "Old Time Rock And Roll.

323. What temperature is mentioned in the Talking Heads tune "Burning Down The House?"

324. How many tracks from Bruce Springsteen's "Born In The U.S.A." album landed in the Billboard top ten.

325. In 1974 at the zenith of their popularity, Led Zeppelin formed their own record label. What did they name it?

326. Who was shot to death outside of his apartment building in New York City on December 8th 1980?

327. What bay area group was looking for a "New Drug" in 1984?

328. What New York quartet warned us about the "Cult Of Personality" in 1989?

329. In 1972 the band Looking Glass made us all fall for a girl without really telling us anything about her. Other than singing that she is "A fine girl," and that "Her eyes could steal a sailor from the sea," we are given no other description of her. We are left to imagine her hair, her height, the way she dresses along with the color of those aforementioned, extraordinary eyes. And perhaps that is why she was so popular. She was whatever we imagined her to be. We remember her name though, don't we?

323. 365 degrees.

324. Seven.

325. Swan Song.

326. John Lennon.

327. Thinking it over, there were probably quite a few of them. But, specifically, Huey Lewis And The News.

328. Living Colour.

329. Brandy.

330. Legend has it that Allen Collins of Lynyrd Skynyrd was asked of his girlfriend, "If I leave here tomorrow, would you still remember me?" Collins used this as the opening line of what song.

331. In what Rick Derringer song does he mention "...A band called the Jokers, they were laying it down?"

332. Bob Dylan wrote a song about a certain Eskimo and Manfred Mann turned it into a top ten hit. Who might this Eskimo be?

333. This artist's successful solo career came after he performed in such groups as Traffic, Blind Faith and The Spencer Davis Group. Name this popular guy.

334. Is there a Fleetwood Mac song that tells of "...A place down in Mexico where a man can fly over mountains and hills?"

335. He was born Marvin Lee Aday, but he adopted the title of a dubious ground beef based dinner entree. Can you name him?

336. In Don Henley's "Boys Of Summer," what apocryphal sign did he see on a Cadillac?

330. "Free Bird."

331. "Rock And Roll Hoochie Koo."

332. That would be "Quinn The Eskimo."

333. Steve Winwood.

334. Yes. It is called "Hypnotized."

335. Meatloaf.

336. A Dead Head Sticker.

337. What song did Eric Clapton write to help him deal with the tragic death of his son?

338. What singer/songwriter went from studying literature at the University of Copenhagen, to penning the immortal lines; "You're the cutest thing that I ever did see. Really love you're peaches, want to shake you're tree?"

339. Do you know Motley Crue member Vince Neil's actual last name?

340. Ian Hunter fronted what group that busted out "All The Young Dudes" in 1972?

341. According to The Eagles, "Somebody's gonna hurt someone, before the night is through. Somebody's gonna come undone, there's nothing we can do." Why?

342. What member of Crosby, Stills and Nash was a co-founding member of The Hollies?

343. "Rock Of Ages," "Foolin'" and "Photograph." Name the album.

337. "Tears In Heaven."

338. Steve Miller.

339. Wharton.

340. Mott The Hoople.

341. Because "There's gonna be a 'Heartache Tonight'."

342. Graham Nash.

343. Pyromania. (Def Leppard.)

344. What Rocker received his Knighthood on December 12th 2003?

345. The last Grateful Dead concert that featured Jerry Garcia happened on July 9th 1995 at what venue?

346. In 1973, the Doobie Brothers sang of "...A sleepy little town down around San Antone'." What is this little town?

347. Name the 1968 Animals number that concerns a military chaplin.

348. What is U2 frontman Bono's real name?

349. Which Rolling Stones album featured a working zipper on the cover?

350. "Gypsy Eyes," "Crosstown Traffic" and "Voodoo Child (Sleight Return.)" Name the album.

344. Sir. Michael Phillip(Mick) Jagger.

345. Soldier Field, Chicago,Ill.

346. "China Grove."

347. "Sky Pilot."

348. Paul David Hewson.

349. "Sticky Fingers."

350. "Electric Ladyland." (Jimi Hendrix.)

351. What Rock album was the first to feature the printed song lyrics?

352. According to The Rolling Stones, where is "...The squirming dog who once had her day?"

353. Which Led Zeppelin album cover art work featured a rotating card wheel known as a Volvelle?

354. Mike Campbell, Benmont Tench, Ron Blair and Stan Lynch comprise the caddish backup band for this Gainesville Florida ladies man?

355. Who provided the guitar work for Robert Plant's 1988 offering "Tall Cool One?"

356. What progressive Rock group took it's name from an eighteenth century agriculturist?

357. In the 1987 film "Light Of Day,"Joan Jett played the leader of what fictional band?

351. "Sgt. Peppers Lonely Hearts Club Band."

352. "Under My Thumb."

353. Led Zeppelin III.

354. They are Tom Petty's 'Heartbreakers'.

355. Jimmy Page.

356. Jethro Tull.

357. "The Barbusters."

358. John Lennon's peace anthem "Imagine" was recorded with the help of what band?

359. Brett Michaels, C.C. Deville, Rikki Rocket and Bobby Dall formed what toxic quartet?

360. What group gave us a 'power' full remake of the T. Rex favorite "Bang A Gong" in 1985? (Although they called their version "Get It On.")

361. Who's last live performance took place in Indianapolis Indiana on June 26th 1977?

362. To what band did guitarist Robin Trower owe his allegiance to from 1968 to 1971?

363. What group gave their 'Royal' treatment to the "Flash Gordon" movie soundtrack in 1980?

364. Deep Purple members Roger Glover and Richie Blackmore teamed with Ronnie James Dio to form what colorful hard Rock group in the early eighties?

358. The Plastic Ono Band.

359. Poison.

360. The Power Station.

361. Elvis Presley.

362. Procol Harum.

363. Queen.

364. Rainbow.

365. What Detroit based Rock outfit brought us such numbers as "Get Ready," "(I Know) I'm Loosing You" and "I Just Want To Celebrate," among others?

366. This singer/songwriter was known as Louis Firbank, then he took his act "Underground" and became better known as who?

367. What Rock quartet exhorted us to "Stand in the place where you live?"

368. For what 80's Rock Quintet did Kevin Cronin sing lead vocals?

369. Which member of the Rolling Stones drowned in July of 1969?

370. In a 1983 ditty, Todd Rundgren wanted to eschew work so that he could play what instrument all day?

371. Alex Lifeson, Neil Peart and Geddy Lee form what Canadian power Rock trio?

365. Rare Earth.

366. Lou Reed.

367. R.E.M.

368. REO Speedwagon.

369. Guitarist Brian Jones.

370. The Drums.

371. Rush.

372. In 1978 the Patti Smith Group saw success with a song co-written be Bruce Springsteen. Name the song?

373. What hard Rock outfit from Hanover Germany formed in 1965 and has sold over 75 million albums world wide?

374. In what Bob Seger confessional does he tell of "Trying to lose those awkward teenage blues?"

375. This Toronto hard Rock foursome told of doing "18 And Life" in a 1989 number. Who might they be?

376. According to the 1979 Sniff 'n The Tears offering "Drivers Seat," what were they doing on a Saturday night?

377. Which ex Beatle displayed his neolithic tendencies in the 1981 film "Caveman?"

378. What former member of The Buffalo Springfield suggested that you "Love The One Your With?"

372. "Because The Night."

373. The Scorpions.

374. "Night Moves."

375. Skid Row.

376. "A little jiving."

377. Ringo Starr.

378. Stephen Stills.

379. Name the hard Rock band that regaled us with an alb named "Dookie?"

380. In 1979, Supertramp warned us... "Better watch what you say they'll be calling you a radical, liberal, fanatical, criminal." In what song?

381. The band Survivor scored a mega-hit by singing of what certain anatomical feature of a ferocious feline?

382. According to the band Sweet, "The man in the back said everyone attack!" Then what happened?

383. On their "Daylight Again" album, Crosby, Stills and Nash sing a tune named for what southern hemisphere constellation?

384. What did the band Ten Years After inform us that they would love to change?

385. Which Van Zant brother sang lead vocals for the band 38 Special?

379. Green Day.

380. "The Logical Song."

381. "The Eye Of The Tiger."

382. "It Turned Into A Ballroom Blitz."

383. "The Southern Cross."

384. The "World."

385. Donnie Van Zant.

386. In a Paul McCartney And Wings song, who is "Stuck inside these four walls. Sent inside forever?"

387. What is the real name of U2 guitarist "The Edge?"

388. According to a Doors song, what have they got out "Back of the Roadhouse...?"

389. With what band did Ringo Starr record prior to joining the Beatles?

390. Born John Waldo, this leader of the bay area group The Tubes is better known by what handle?

391. What British hard Rock band took the name of the villainous lawyer in the Dickens tome "David Copperfield?"

392. What two hard Rock brothers were born in Nijmegen, The Netherlands before moving to Pasadena, Ca. In 1968?

386. The "Band On The Run."

387. Dave Evans.

388. "...Some bungalows."

389. Rory Storm And The Hurricanes.

390. Fee Waybill.

391. Uriah Heep.

392. Alex and Eddie Van Halen.

393. What 1973 'Who' Rock opera became a movie in 1979?

394. Who did Neil Young have as backup singers on his number one hit song "Heart Of Gold?"

395. Frank Beard, Dusty Hill and Billy Gibbons form the Texas Rock trio ZZ Top. Which member is known for not having a beard?

396. According to his song, Tommy Tutone found a certain phone number on the wall telling him "For a good time call." What was that number again?

397. There were at least three names for the group that eventually became The Beatles. Can you recount any of those names?

398. What Doors hit did Jim Morrison say he wrote after observing a thin young black girl walking along Venice beach?

399. What 1966 Stones number was concerned with the passive drug abuse of the modern housewife?

393. "Quadrophenia."

394. James Taylor and Linda Ronstadt.

395. Frank Beard.

396. 867-5309.

397. "The Quarrymen," "Johnny And The Moondogs" and "The Silver Beatles." Those are the only names my research can find. Any of those are acceptable.

398. "Hello, I Love You."

399. "Mothers Little Helper."

400. Special Discussion Question.

If you had to choose one tune to represent Rock and Roll music in a cultural time capsule that would not be opened for a thousand years or so, what Rock tune would you choose? (This authors choice is "Layla" by Derek And The Dominoes.) Grab some chips and salsa and discuss this at length.

401. Before grabbing a mike stand as a Rock vocal sensation, Rod Stewart grabbed a shovel while engaging in what dead end job?

402. What modern twist on an ancient Asian medical art does Eric Clapton site as helping him overcome his heroin addiction?

403. What was the title of Led Zeppelins fourth album?

404. Which Pink Floyd album has a photo of a man on fire on the front cover?

405. What prominent American Rock band took a "Permanent Vacation" in 1987?

406."Juke Box Hero," "Girl On The Moon" and "Urgent." Name the album.

400. It's a discussion question. You'll find no answers here.

401. Gravedigger.

402. "Electro" Acupuncture.

403. The album had neither a title nor a band name on the cover. However, it was commonly known as Led Zeppelin IV.

404. "Wish You Were Here."

405. Aerosmith.

406. "Foreigner 4."

407. From a Stealers Wheel number, if there are "Clowns to the left of me," and "Jokers to the right," then where am I?

408. The last three words heard in the Doors tune "Touch Me" are "Stronger than dirt." Where did that phrase originate?

409. Janis Joplin sings, "I'd trade all my tomorrows for one single yesterday,"to be doing what?

410. In the first verse of Steely Dan's "Do It Again," the character in the song has apparently been convicted of murder. Yet, he is put back on the street. Why?

411. Did Elvis Presley have a twin brother?

412. According to their 1979 album title, where was Supertramp having breakfast?

413. "Rat Salad," "Iron Man" and "War Pigs." Name the album.

407. "Stuck In The Middle With You."

408. Ajax Cleanser commercials.

409. "Holding Bobby's body next to mine."

410. Because "...The hangman isn't hanging."

411. Yes. On January 8th 1935, his twin brother, Jessie Garon Presley, was delivered stillborn. Elvis arrived, quite healthy, 35 minutes later. Jesse was buried the next day.

412. In America.

413. "Paranoid." (Black Sabbath.)

414. How old was guitar virtuoso and Ozzy Osbourne axeman Randy Rhodes when he died?

415. In an AC/DC ditty, what does the phone number 362-4360 get you?

416. Who succeeded Denny Laine as the vocalist for the Moody Blues?

417. What west coast psychedelic group improved their aroma with "Incense And Peppermints?"

418. what singer/songwriter/guitarist was featured in such films as "Eat The Document," "Don't Look Back," "Hearts Of Fire" and "Pat Garret And Billy The Kid?"

419. Who provided keyboard accompaniment for the Beatles on their recordings of "Get Back" and Let It Be?"

420. The band Lynyrd Skynyrd formed while in high school in Jacksonville Florida. They adapted their name after one of their teachers, Leonard Skinner. What did Mr. Skinner teach?

414. 25 years old.

415. "Dirty Deeds Done Dirt Cheap."

416. Justin Hayward.

417. Strawberry Alarm Clock.

418. Bob Dylan.

419. Billy Preston.

420. Gym.

421. These 70's hit makers decided on their name after reading an article that told of indigenous Australians that would sleep with wild Dingos for extra warmth on cold nights. If the night was very cold, one might sleep with two, maybe three Dingos. Can you name this group?

422. In the Bryan Adams song "Summer Of '69," he tells of a band composed of "Me and some guys from school..." that fell apart. What happened to band members Jimmy and Jody?

423. What Australian new wave/Rock combo was formed by the Farriss brothers in 1977?

424. A Kansas number says, "I hear the voices when I'm dreaming, I can hear them say..." Say what?

425. With album sales that far exceeded the standard for the music industry's Gold Album Award, Iron Butterfly's "In-A-Gadda-Da-Vida" album was the first to receive an album award struck in a different precious metal. Name the metal.

426. Is there a Marshall Tucker in The Marshall Tucker Band?

427. In "Bohemian Rhapsody," Queen beseeches "Bismillah" to "Let him go." Who or what is Bismillah?

421. Three Dog Night.

422. "Jimmy quit and Jody got married."

423. INXS.

424. "Carry On My Wayward Son."

425. Platinum.

426. No. The name Marshall Tucker was taken from the logo of a piano tuning company.

427. Bismillah is an Arabic phrase that means "In the name of god."

428. What Parker Brothers board game is mentioned in the Sting solo effort "Seven Days?"

429. What legendary British band's first compilation, or best of, album was titled, "Meaty Beaty Big And Bouncy?"

430. What was the first KISS album cover to show the gang without their trademark face makeup?

431. What character from the "Wizard Of Oz" ended up in the title of a song by the group America?

432. Where in his body was the cancer that eventually took ex Beatle George Harrison from us?

433. "Two Out Of Three Ain't Bad," "For Crying Out Loud" and "Paradise By The Dashboard Lights." Name the album.

434. In 1988, what Atlanta quartet admonished us with, "Don't tell me no lies and keep your hands to yourself?"

428. Scrabble.

429. The Who.

430. 1983's "Lick It Up."

431. The :Tin Man."

432. His Throat.

433. Bat Out Of Hell. (Meat Loaf.)

434. The Georgia Satellites.

435. From whom did Michael McDonald take over the Doobie Brothers lead vocal duties?

436. The Eagles sing of a road with how many bridges on it.

437. George Young, the older brother of AC/DC's Malcom and Angus Young, played guitar in an Australian band that had "Friday" on their mind. Can you name this distracted quintet?

438. The subject of the Pink Floyd song "Comfortably Numb" is assured that there will be no more "AARRRRGGGGGGG!" after he feels what?

439. In the Jefferson Airplane psychedelic classic :White Rabbit," in what odd manner is the "White Knight" mentioned as talking?

440. Considering the band E.L.O., what does E.L.O. Stand for?

441. What band finally got to see their smiling faces on "The Cover Of The Rolling Stone" on March 29th 1973?

435. Tom Johnston.

436. Seven.

437. The Easybeats.

438. "Just a little pin prick."

439. Backwards.

440. The Electric Light Orchestra.

441. Dr. Hook And The Medicine Show.

442. According to Emerson, Lake and Palmer's "Karn Evil 9 – First Impression. Part 2," we are told, "Performing on a stool we've a sight to make you drool. What is that sight?

443. Ia 1966 Stones hit, what color do they suggest that a "Red Door" be painted?

444. What Australian hard Rock guitarist adapted his signature school uniform outfit form the uniform he wore at Ashfield Boys High School in Sydney?

445. From a 1971 Traffic offering, "But today you just read that the man was shot dead by a gun that didn't make any noise. But it wasn't the bullet that laid him to rest..." What was it?

446. What art Rock band originated at the Rhode Island school of design?

447. Who did Kieth Moon replace as the original drummer of "The Who?"

448. In what city was the band America formed?

442. "Seven virgins on a mule."

443. Black.

444. Angus Young.

445. It "...Was the low spark of high heeled boys."

446. The Talking Heads.

447. Doug Sandom. He was the original drummer, until he was replaced by Moon in 1964.

448. London England.

449. In 1965, famous brothers Gregg and Duane Allman formed a group with a name very like that of a candy bar. What was that tasty band name?

450. Who is Steven Tallarico better known as?

451. Apart from David Lee Roth and Sammy Hagar, who else has provided lead vocals for the band Van Halen?

452. Where did Sammy Hagar earn the nickname "The Red Rocker?"

453. Who did the Rolling Stones feature as the female guest vocalist for their classic number "Gimme Shelter?"

454. What was the name of Pat Benatar's controversial song about abused kids?

455. According to the Paul McCartney and Wings song "Band On The Run," what did the first one say to the second one there?

449. The Allman Joys.

450. Aerosmith lead vocalist Steven Tyler.

451. Gary Cherone. (On "Van Halen III.")

452. From his early solo single appropriately entitled "Red."

453. Merry Clayton.

454. Hell Is For Children.

455. "I hope your having fun."

456. In the Cream number "Strange Brew," what is it that the Strange Brew will do?

457. Z.Z.Top tells us, "I lake the enchiladas and the teriyaki too. I even like the chicken if the sauce is not to blue." What is the source of these delightful meals?

458. Neil Young And Crazy Horse confide a brutal act that happened "Down By The River." What happened?

459. In a Stones song, "*He...*" "*...Rode a tank, held a generals rank, when the blitzkreig raged and the bodies stank.*" Who is "*He?*"

460. What Beatles album featured the hit song "Penny Lane?"

461. Blue Oyster Cult tells us that "Seasons" don't fear him, nor do the "...Wind or the sun or the rain." Who is he?

462. In the Cheap Trick song "Surrender," we learn that mommy served with the W.A.C.S. During the 'war.' Where was she stationed?

456. Kill what's inside of you.

457. T.V. Dinners.

458. "I shot my baby."

459. The Devil.

560. None. Although recoded during the Sgt. Pepper sessions, it was released as a double A sided single along with the song "Strawberry Fields."

461. The Reaper.

462. The Philippines.

463. From Bob Dylan's "Like A Rolling Stone," "You used to ride on a chrome horse with your diplomat." What did that diplomat carry on his shoulder?

464. Who was the bass player for Led Zeppelin?

465. What is the next line in this sequence from the Pink Floyd number "Hey You." "But it was only a fantasy. The wall was too high as you can see. No matter how he tried he could not break free...?"

466. In what Led Zeppelin song do we hear, "Talk and songs from tongues of lilting grace, who's sounds caress my ear?"

467. Where is it that Joe Walsh tells us that "...Nothing grows and life ain't very pretty. No one's there to catch you when you fall?"

468. In the Doors offering "Moonlight Drive," where does Jim Morrison suggest that he and his unnamed companion swim to?

469. What band wound up and threw strikes with their 1998 hit album "All The Pain Money Can Buy?"

463. A Siamese Cat.

464. John Paul Jones.

465. "And the worms ate into his brain."

466. "Kashmir."

467. "In The City."

468, The Moon. Of course.

469. Fastball.

470. In what song does Fleetwwod Mac warn us , "But don't ask me what I think of you I might not give the answer that you want me to?"

471. In the Stones song "Gimme Shelter," Mick Jagger sings of something being "...Just a shot away." What is that something?

472. "Bullet The Blue Sky," "Red Hill Mining Town" and "With Or Without You." Name the album.

473. According to Commander Cody and his Lost Planet Airmen, "My pappy said 'Son, you're gonna drive me to drinkin' if you don't stop..." Stop what?

474. according to and Eric Clapton tune, about what time are we "...Gonna cause talk and suspicion, gonna give an exhibition,...gonna find out what it is all about?"

475. In the Supertramp track "Breakfast In America," what is the singers opinion of his girlfriend?

476. Speaking of which, how did the band Supertramp come upon such a name?

470. "Oh Well."

471. War.

472. The Joshua Tree. (U2.)

473. "Drivin' that Hot Rod Lincoln."

474. "After Midnight."

475. She's "Not much of a girlfriend."

476. From the 1908 W.H. Davies novel "The Autobiography Of A Super-Tramp."

477. Who was the final performer at the Woodstock Music and art Fair in August 1969.

478. What type of 'Boy' did Foreigner sing of in a 1979 hit?

479. "Woodstock," "Helpless" and "Teach Your Children." name the album.

480. Name the guitar legend who's signature line of guitars include such specimen as the "Wolfgang" and the "Frankenstein."

481. The 1980 book "No One Here Gets Out Alive," by Jerry Hopkins and Danny Sugarman, chronicles what Rock and Roll frontman?

482. What famous Pin Up artist came out of retirement to provide the illustration for the cars album "Candy-O?"

483. The album photo on the cover of the Eagles "Hotel California" depicts what iconic California hotel?

477. Jimi Hendrix.

478. A "Dirty White Boy."

479. "Deja Vu." (Crosby, Stills, Nash and Young.)

480. Eddie Van Halen.

481. Jim Morrison.

482. Alberto Vargas.

483. The Beverly Hills Hotel.

484. What group served up a heaping helping of "Brain Salad Surgery" in 1973.

485. What gracious, but macabre salutation did Alice Cooper offer us with the title of his 1975 album?

486. Vincent Damon Furnier is better known as what theatrical Rocker?

487. According to Huey Lewis And The News, what is still beating in such places as "D.C, San Antone, The Liberty Town, Boston and Baton rouge. Tulsa, Austin, Oklahoma City, Seattle, San Francisco too?"

488. Who did the Eagles tell to "Come to your senses, come down from your fences."in a 1973 song?

489. Who played the bass for the Rolling Stones from 1962 to 1992?

490. According to Pink Floyd's "The Happiest Days Of Their Lives," what did their "Fat and psychopathic wives" do to "Certain teachers" when they got home at night?

484. Emerson, Lake and Palmer.

485. Welcome To My Nightmare.

486. Alice Cooper.

487. "The Heart Of Rock And Roll."

488. "Desperado."

489. Bill Wyman.

490. "...Thrash them within inches of their lives."

491. In what Creedence Clearwater Revival song are we warned, "My dady said 'Son don't let the man get ya and do what he done to me?'"

492. On what Doors track do you hear this exchange?
"Father?"
"Yes Son?"
"I want to kill you."

493. In the Rod Stewart offering "Every Picture Tells A Story," where is Rod when he tells us, "My body stunk, but I kept my funk?"

494. His given name is Fred Bulsara and he once recorded under the name Larry Lurex. Who is he better known as?

495. In a 1981 song, The Clash wonder, "Should I Stay Or Should I Go." What do they tell us are the consequences of either decision?

496. In the Van Halen track "Ain't Talkin' 'Bout Love," David Lee Roth tells of a place he has been where he has lost a lot of friends. What is this place?

497. In the Rock musical "Hair," the character Claude Bukowski is in New York city for a last few days before he does what?

491. "Born On The Bayou."

492. "The End."

493. Rome.

494. Freddy Mercury.

495. "If I stay there will be trouble. If I go it will be double."

496. The Edge.

497. Enlist in the Army.

498. In the Aerosmith song "Dream On," how long are we encouraged to dream on?

499. In what hit song does Steve Miller champion the causes of the underprivileged and the homeless?

500. In a Chuck Berry early Rock classic, who used to "...Carry his guitar in a gunny sack and sit beneath the trees by the railroad track?"

501.What was the last track on the last album the Beatles recorded?

498. Until your dreams come true.

499. "Fly Like An Eagle."

500. "Johnny B. Goode.

501. "The End." (Abbey Road. Their last recorded album.)